Meand...

1 Ironbridge Iron Gorge

2 Blist Hill via Lloyds Coppice

3 Benthall Edge via Severn Valley Way

4 Coalport

5 Shifnal

6 Albrighton

7 Much Wenlock

8 Beckbury

9 Wrekin

10 Tong

DISCLAIMER

The contents of the book are correct at time of publication. However, we cannot be held responsible for any errors or omissions or changes in details or for any consequences of any reliance on the information provided. We have tried to be accurate in the book, but things can change and would be grateful if readers advise me of any inaccuracies they may encounter.

I have taken every care to ensure the walks are safe and achievable by walkers with a reasonable level of fitness. But with outdoor activities there is always a degree of risk involved and the publisher accepts no responsibility for any injury caused to readers while following these walks.

SAFETY FIRST

All the walks have been covered to ensure minimum risk to walkers that follow the routes.

Always be particularly careful if crossing main roads, but remember traffic can also be dangerous even on minor country lanes.

If in the country and around farms be careful of farm machinery and livestock (take care to put dog on lead) and observe the **Country Code**.

Also ensure you wear suitable clothing and footwear, I would advise wearing walking boots which protect from wet feet and add extra ankle support over uneven terrain.

There are a few rules that should be observed if walking alone advises somebody were you are walking and approximate time you will return. Allow plenty of time for the walk especially if it is further and or more difficult than you have walked before. Whatever the distance be sure you have enough daylight hours to complete the walk safely. When walking along a country road always walk on the right to face oncoming traffic, the only exception is on a blind bend where you cross to the left to have a clear view and can be seen from both directions.

If bad weather should come in making visibility difficult, do not panic just try to remember any features along route and get out the map to pinpoint the area but be sure before you move off, that you are moving in the right direction.

Unfortunately, accidents can still happen even on the easiest of walks, if this is the case make sure the person in trouble is safe before seeking help. If carrying a mobile phone dial 999 or 112 European Union emergency number will connect you to any network to get you help.

Unmapped walks we recommend that you take the relevant Ordnance Survey map and compass with you, even if you have a Smartphone, digi-walker or G.P.S all of which can fail on route.

Introduction

Shropshire was once the start and the heart of the Industrial Revelation. The historic and the cultural landscapes in Shropshire are quite unique. Dispute its Industrial past it still as upland heather moors and fertile lowlands linked with the hedgerows. The River Severn also meanders its way through Shropshire flowing under the magnificent Ironbridge. The village Ironbridge takes its name from the famous Iron Bridge a 30-metre cast iron bridge built spanning the River Severn, which enable the village to develop alongside the bridge. It was Abraham Darby who built the bridge by perfecting the technique of smelting the iron with coke in Coalbrookdale which allowed a cheaper production on iron. But even though it had a busy Industrial past Shropshire now as 50 designated wild places and over 37 nature reserves. Shropshire is very keen to welcome walkers and there are currently ten towns across Shropshire that have gained Walkers Welcome status.

This book contains ten circular walks with step by step easy to follow instructions, there are routes over the Wrekin, Much Wenlock and Tong to mention just a few all of which have their views and interesting sites along the walk. The book sets out to help persuade you to spend more time to explore the rich diverse environment that exists beyond its Industrial heritage and museums of the Iron Gorge. The walks have been specially selected to provide walkers with a variation in landscape and vistas of some of the most excellent countryside in the U.K. The Iron Gorge is a particularly nice example of a reclaimed industrial site which has been transformed back to nature. It now provides a unique and beautiful wooded valley, this leaves the Gorge covered with a network of footpaths, bridleways and country lanes. Once you go beyond the Iron Gorge you have the sheer beauty of Shropshire to explore, with its medieval towns, spectacular scenery and the historical sites that date back over 2,000 years.

Please remember when going out on a walk to leave information with someone where you have gone and if possible how long? Also, check the walk with a O.S. map do not put all your faith in G.P.S or Smartphone, and be sure to pack food and drink for the trip there may not be any cafes or pubs. On most of these walks the ground is uneven and some areas very steep so take care when wet there could be a risk of slipping, always wear your walking boots for wet and muddy conditions which will also give you that extra support to protect the ankles and feet from damage.

Happy Walking

Meandering in Shropshire

Chapter 1 Ironbridge via Iron Gorge

Park & Start Grid ref; SJ 672032

Distance: 3 miles

Level; Strenuous

Time: 2 hours

Terrain: Pavements, pathways open fields and woodland.

Maps. O.S Explorer 242 Telford, Ironbridge and The Wrekin

Refreshments Tea Emporium.

Iron Bridge opened in 1781.

River Severn from the Ironbridge.

Access to start

Leave M54 at junction 4 up the slip road to go off at 2nd exit onto A464. Then go through two roundabouts still on the A464 and at the next roundabout take 1st exit then take slip road onto A442 Queensway. Follow to next roundabout take the 1st exit onto A4373 Castlefield Way, then pass through a further two roundabouts onto Madeley Road to arrive in Ironbridge where there is plenty of car parks.

Places Nearby

Ironbridge

This is a great place to explore for history and museums, it is a quaint village on the River Severn at the heart of the Ironbridge Gorge. It was the birthplace of the industrial revolution, this was all because of Abraham Darby who perfected the technique of smelting iron with coke in Coalbrookdale, this allowed industry to manufacture much cheaper production of iron.

The Walk

(1)

The walk starts at the car park just off the end of Bridge Road. Exit car park and turn right to go past the Old Toll House and then carry on across the famous Iron Bridge. Once over the bridge, turn left to continue down what is known as the Wharfage with the River Severn on your left. Stay on the Wharfage for about a half mile to reach a mini roundabout, turn right on into Dale Road which is signposted Coalbrookdale Museum. Continue up Dale Road following the pavement on the left past the primary school and then on past Trinity Hall which is now a doctor's surgery with the original Coalbrookdale cast iron lamp post outside by the gateway.

(2)

Then from here continue uphill on past the Upper Forge area on the right with a picnic area if you wish to stop. If not then carry on up the road still on the pavement on the left to where the road changes name to Paradise, at this point cross over the road to the opposite side to follow a footpath between houses with a way marker sign. Continue up the steps between the houses to the Holy Trinity Church, near the top of the hill and then follow the path around the church to exit via the cast iron side gate out onto Church Road. Cross over the road carefully and enter Dale Coppice woods, from here take the path up the steps and follow the finger post marked with the red arrows. Then carry on along the boardwalk on the left to stay on the path ahead, from here just follow the red route for the rest of the trail. Be sure to look at the information markers as to where Doric Temple stood and Hannah's Garden was once positioned.

(3)

Then soon after reaching the top you will leave the woodland via a kissing gate to enter Rough Park. Turn right in the park to follow the path with Dale Coppice on the right, continue down the path to the right to go through another gate onto a track. Then stay on the track taking advantage of the magnificent views, keep around to the right on the track to finally reach a metal gate that leads out onto Church Road.

(4)

Cross the road taking care of traffic and follow the finger post to The Rotunda which goes on to enter Lincoln Hill via a kissing gate. Continue past an alcove where there was once a seat with a view out over the valley. The path then comes out of the woodland to a fenced grassy section with the River Severn about 120 metres below. Then follow the trail on down 200 steps **(Yes 200)** to the bottom where you turn right to follow the finger post, then bear left down another flight of steps.

(5)

Then turn left with a house wall on the right, carry on down to Lincoln Hill Road, cross over road onto a public footpath go down the hill to reach the Wharfage, turn left and then simply retrace your steps on back to the car park.

Chapter 2 Blist Hill via Lloyd's Coppice

Park & Start Grid ref; SJ 682033

Distance: 2 miles

Level; Moderate

Time: 1 hours 15 minutes

Terrain: Pavements, pathways and woodland.

Maps. O.S Explorer 242 Telford, Ironbridge and The Wrekin

Refreshments Ironbridge or Coalport.

Lloyds Coppice.

Track near the Ice House.

Access to start

Leave the M54 motorway at junction 4, then take 2nd exit onto A464 Priorslee Road continue through 2 roundabouts still on the A464. Then at the next roundabout take the 1st exit to merge onto the A442 Queensway, then take slip road on A4169 to Madeley/Shifnal and at next roundabout take 4th exit A4269 Kemberton Road. Still on the A4169 at roundabout take 2nd exit and again at next roundabout 2nd exit onto Legges Way and then turn right onto Coalport Road follow road to bottom of hill turn right along road next to River Severn past The Lloyds to reach a layby on the left, if you go too far you reach the bridge B4373 turn and head back about 300 metres to layby now on right.

Places Nearby

Blist Hill Victorian Town

This attraction is nearby to the walk, Blist Hill is an open-air museum it contains buildings from the industrial site, and buildings like Victorian Sweet Shop with other replica buildings which have been restored and relocated to the museum. There is also the New Inn public house which was originally between Green Lane and Hospital Street Walsall. All the workers on site are in costume and have been trained in the skills and history of the profession they re-enact.

The Walk

(1)

The walk starts at the small layby on the road to Coalport, just of the junction of the new bridge into Jackfield. Exit the layby and carefully cross the road to go through a gate into Lloyds Coppice. Then once in the woods follow the finger posts to navigate through the woods to reach a junction with straight ahead to the Ice House and Coalport, or left uphill to Blist Hill.

(2)

Go left and climb uphill continue to follow the trail to Blist Hill, to finally exit out onto Coalport Road. At this point you can cross the road near the Blist Hill Victorian Town to locate the Silkin Way trail or alternatively just follow the Coalport Road down to the bottom road junction. The Silkin Way runs parallel with the road and towards the bottom of the hill keep right to exit out on to Coalport Road.

(3)

Down at the road junction with a triangle of grass in the centre keep around to the right, then cross over the road again to walk along the pavement next to the River Severn in the direction away from Coalport. Continue to follow the pavement for almost a mile to finally reach the layby set back on the left to the parked car.

Chapter 3 Benthall Edge via Severn Valley Way

Park & Start Grid ref; SJ 672032

Distance: 2 miles

Level; Strenuous

Time: 1 hours 45 minutes

Terrain: Part of Severn Valley Way, on disused Severn Valley rail track woodland paths.

Maps. O.S Explorer 242 Telford, Ironbridge and The Wrekin

Refreshments Ironbridge.

Trail through the woods.

Old Pattern's Rock Quarry face.

Access to start

Leave the M54 motorway at junction 4, then take 2nd exit onto A464 Priorslee Road continue through 2 roundabouts still on the A464. Then at the next roundabout take the 1st exit to merge onto the A442 Queensway, take slip road on A4169 to Madeley/Shifnal and at next roundabout take 4th exit A4269 Kemberton Road. Then still on the A4169 at roundabout take 2nd exit and again at next roundabout 2nd exit onto Legges Way and turn right onto Coalport Road follow road to bottom of hill turn right along road next to River Severn past The Lloyds to reach the bridge on left over the River Severn onto the B4373 and follow round to car park in Bridge Road next to the Iron Bridge and Toll House.

Places Nearby

Benthall House National Trust

Benthall is a small estate, but packed with things to do. Visit the house and stroll through the gardens, pop in for tea and cakes at the tea room and continue with a walk through the park and woods. The house is still tenanted by the Benthall family today, and they can trace their lineage back to the Saxon period on the site.

The Walk

(1)

The walk starts at the Station Yard car park off Bridge Road. Exit car park and turn left going away from the Ironbridge, then walk for about 10 metres to turn right onto the Old Severn Valley Railway Track. Continue along the track for about 200 metres before turning left through a gate then continue to climb up the steps signposted Broseley, go on to the next signpost and carry on following the track in the direction of Broseley. This is quite a trek uphill along a lot of steps which can take 20 minutes or more to reach the top.

(2)

Once at the top keep over to the right and follow the signpost marked with red. Once at the next finger post follow the track marked Pattern's Rock Quarry **(PRQ)** which passes over two wooden bridges taking you across Bower Brook that flows all the way down to the River Severn. Stay on track and continue onto the next finger post turn right and follow the path uphill and then at the next finger post turn right to the Pattern's Rock Quarry viewing point.

(3)

Now you start the descent of Benthall Edge by following the steps down the hill. At the next bench stop to enjoy the great view out over Coalbrookdale Valley. Then carry on and once at the bottom of the long flight of steps turn right and follow signpost marked Ironbridge. Just continue to follow this still high pathway with views out over the River Severn and the Old Severn Valley Railway Track down below **(this section can be very muddy)**. Then as you continue to follow the path you start to drop down reaching an area of many tracks, at this point keep over to the left to get onto to the Old disused Severn Valley Railway Track and then retrace your steps back to the Station Yard car park.

Chapter 4 Coalport

Park & Start Grid ref; SJ 695024

Distance: 3 miles

Level; Easy

Time: 1 hours 15 minutes

Terrain: Part of Severn Valley Way, Silkin Way and country roads.

Maps. O.S Explorer 242 Telford, Ironbridge and The Wrekin

Refreshments Woodbridge Inn.

Shropshire Canal Coalport.

The Leaning House

Access to start

Leave the M54 motorway at junction 4, then take 2nd exit onto A464 Priorslee Road continue through 2 roundabouts still on the A464. Then at the next roundabout take the 1st exit to merge onto the A442 Queensway, then take slip road on A4169 to Madeley/Shifnal and at next roundabout take 4th exit A4269 Kemberton Road. Still on the A4169 at roundabout take 2nd exit and again at next roundabout 2nd exit onto Legges Way and then turn right onto Coalport Road follow road to bottom of hill and turn left to arrive in Coalport park in museum car park or a layby on the left nearby.

Places Nearby

Coalport China Museum

Explore the buildings that were home to the famous Coalport China Factory until 1926. Look at the distinctive bottle shaped chimneys of the two surviving bottle ovens. Then watch live demonstrations of traditional techniques in flower making, pot throwing and china painting.

The Walk

(1)

The walk starts at the small parking area up the slope on left at the side of the road just before reaching the Coalport China Museum. Exit car park and turn left then walk past the Coalport China Museum via a short section of the Shropshire Canal known as the Coalport Canal, emerge back out onto the road and continue to reach a small bridge. Then just before the bridge crossover the road and turn right onto the Silkin Way trail go under the bridge and continue for 600 metres to reach road junction at Coalport Road.

(2)

Turn right onto Coalport Road crossing over Coalport Bridge, then just over the bridge on the left is Woodbridge Inn where you can stop for refreshments. Then continue walk up the road and take the track off to the right on the Severn Valley Way signposted to Ironbridge. The trail then veers to the left up a slope and then at the top the trail then sweeps to the right which then levels out to follow the Old disused railway line. Continue to follow the Old Disused Railway line for about 1.5 miles on past the Salt house properties on the right, stay on the pavement to go past the Jackfield Tile Works to reach a road junction, keep over to the right and cross road to pick-up the Old Disused Rail line again on the other side of road to continue towards Ironbridge.

(3)

Then after about 200 metres and just before going under a bridge turn right up a steep slope to join a path down to a road junction, turn left at junction onto Coalford and then almost immediately turn right onto Jackfield Bridge. Cross over Jackfield Bridge and then at the end turn right on the pavement along The Lloyds, then continue to follow road for about 1.2 miles back into Coalport to return to the car in the parking area.

Chapter 5 Shifnal

Park & Start Grid ref; SJ 749078

Distance: 3 miles

Level; Easy

Time: 1 hours 15 minutes

Terrain: Country lanes and open fields.

Maps. O.S Explorer 242 Telford, Ironbridge and The Wrekin

Refreshments Shifnal.

Open Countryside views.

Driveway to Coppice Green House.

Access to start

Leave M54 motorway at junction 4 exit at 1st turn on roundabout onto A464, then at next roundabout take 3rd exit and follow A464 into Shifnal, at the traffic lights turn left and immediately right drive past pub on left and after 50 metres go left into village hall car park.

Places Nearby

Shrewsbury

Great place to visit with the castle and all the ancient buildings around the town, plenty to do and parking is very good. Come along to see the new and old working together with a fab selection of cafes and bars to enjoy fine wine and excellent food.

The Walk

(1)

The walk starts at the car park next to Shifnal village hall. Exit car park by taking the alleyway down past the Co-Op store onto the High Street in Shifnal town centre. Turn right and walk up the High Street, cross road and then just after Broadway Close take the alleyway on the left to walk down and across the Wesley Brook, then turn right to follow the brook.

(2)

Continue to reach the road ahead, go straight over road on past the children's play area to reach a small bridge. Crossover the bridge and up the path onto road then follow road on up to the main road at the top of slope. Turn left on main road then carefully crossover road, and then after 200 metres bear right on the road, crossover and take the service road to the left to keep the tall hedge to your left. Continue straight ahead along the footpath through the slight wooded area to emerge to re-join the road and continue underneath the M54 motorway bridge.

(3)

Then just under bridge take the path up the bank on the right to stile at the top, cross stile into field to continue to follow path along the right of the field for about 600 metres to reach a wooden bridge.

(4)

Crossover the bridge and then turn left along the next field keeping the hedge now on your left until you reach a stile on the left. Crossover stile then take care to keep to the way marked pathway across the front of the Coppice Green House and continue to reach the lane.

(5)

Then from here turn right, to follow lane as you cross the bridge back over the M54 motorway. Then from here there are pleasant views out over the town ahead and the Shropshire Hills in the distance. Continue back down towards the town centre, going past the new housing estate and football ground on the right and then further on past the school. At the road junction go past the first lane on right to keep over to the right to follow on into Ashton Street to return up road to turn right into car park next to village hall.

Chapter 6 Albrighton

Park & Start Grid ref; SJ 813043

Distance: 3 miles

Level; Easy

Time: 1 hours 15 minutes

Terrain: Country lanes and open fields.

Maps. O.S Explorer 242 Telford, Ironbridge and The Wrekin

Refreshments Albrighton.

Out in the Countryside at Albrighton.

Open scenery just outside Albrighton.

Access to start

Leave M54 motorway at junction 4 exit at 1st turn on roundabout onto A464, then at next roundabout take 3rd exit and follow A464 into Shifnal. Continue through the traffic lights in Shifnal and follow A464 and signpost on into Albrighton to the car park behind the Crown Inn pub.

Places Nearby

Royal Air Museum Cosford

This one of the largest aviation collections in the U.K, with 70 historic aircraft displayed in the ex-wartime hangars. Also, there is the Refuel Restaurant serving hot and cold meals, or check out Checkpoint Charlie Cafe with light snacks and drinks. Just a Great Day out.

The Walk

(1)

The walk starts from the car park behind the Crown Inn pub. Exit car park and cross over the road on the High Street to take the first left down Cross Road. Then continue down the road on the pavement keeping over to the left-hand side. Then just before you get to Newhouse Lane turn left to go through a wooden gate and follow the enclosed path with a wooden fence on the right. Once at the end you reach a housing estate drive, carry straight ahead on drive before keeping over to the left to walk down a narrow gravel path with a wooden fence on your left.

(2)

Carry straight on down the path to reach and go through a metal gate, go straight ahead on the path to then go through another metal gate. Just continue along path, ignore the stile on the right to go through a third metal gate. Stay on the pathway to go through yet a fourth metal gate, then once through the gate you are out on to a wide track. Then once on the wide track turn right and go through a kissing gate after 25 metres to continue along the path to finally reach a footbridge over a stream.

(3)

Once at the footbridge you can shorten the walk by turning left just before the footbridge. But to continue the walk cross the footbridge and on through the field to reach and go through a kissing gate, then carry on up the next field to go through a wooden gate at the end. Then finally on through an enclosed pathway to continue up to a kissing gate, go through a gate out on to Woodhouse Lane.

(4)

Once on Woodhouse Lane, turn left to go past a house called Woodhouse, then as soon has you pass the house turn left to go through a metal gate. Please follow the instructions keeping dogs under control. Once through the gate keep over to the right onto a narrow path to cross a stile on the right to continue to another stile. Go along the field with the hedge on the left, carry on to cross over a footbridge across a stream. Go straight ahead to then cross a stile to continue to go through a kissing gate to emerge out onto a road. Cross the main road carefully to turn left on pavement and follow the path on into Albrighton on past shops to finally reach The Crown Inn pub and car park.

Chapter 7 Much Wenlock

Park & Start Grid ref; SJ 623000

Distance: 3 miles

Level; Easy

Time: 1 hours 15 minutes

Terrain: Country lanes and open fields.

Maps. O.S Explorer 242 Telford, Ironbridge and The Wrekin

Refreshments Much Wenlock.

Wenlock Priory in Much Wenlock.

Lane out of Much Wenlock.

Access to start

Leave the M54 motorway at junction 4, and then exit the roundabout at 2nd exit onto A464 Priorslee Road, pass through a further 2 roundabouts still on the A464. Then at the next roundabout take the 1st exit to merge onto the A442 Queensway and then keep straight ahead on the A4169 Queensway through a further 3 roundabouts to turn left still on the A4169 onto Much Wenlock Road. Then follow road straight through with change of names into Much Wenlock, to follow the signpost to Wenlock Priory to park in the Priory car park.

Places Nearby

Much Wenlock Priory

Much Wenlock Priory is a tranquil ruin of the 12th century, step back in time and soak up the picturesque surroundings just on the outskirts of Much Wenlock. Go for a stroll through the grounds see the Chapter House, Cloister Gardens and the medieval tiles then be sure to visit the Heritage Shop with all its fine souvenirs.

The town that was responsible for the revival of the modern Olympic games in the 19th century.

The Walk

(1)

The walk starts at the car park next to Wenlock Priory. Leave the car park and then walk past the entrance to Wenlock Priory and then continue along the lane ignoring all other footpaths to stay on the lane as it veers around to the right, go down lane for 100 metres and turn left down towards Down's Mill to enter onto Down's Mill driveway (Please keep dogs on lead down drive). Continue past the mill buildings keeping over to the right to follow a narrow footpath. Then cross over the narrow footbridge to go into a field. Once in the field be sure to take the well-defined diagonal path across the field towards a kissing gate.

(2)

Then after going through the kissing gate walk along the left-hand side of the field keeping next to the hedge. Then after a short distance you reach Wykes Road turn left along a section of Jack Mylton Way for a short distance before taking the footpath off to the left, this is just before reaching the main road.

(3)

Now once on the footpath which was once the Old Railway Track follow on back to reach a fork in the track, then at this point where the left turn goes off to the Shropshire Way. But for our walk we continue straight on walking for about 500 metres still staying on the Old Railway Track, continue following the track ignoring all steps with metal rails both on the left and the right.

(4)

Continue the track to the end and follow the path up the slope around to the right and head to the entrance gate. Go through the gate and then turn left to go past the house on your right to follow the track out to a lane. Then walk straight ahead to go past Station House to turn left almost immediately after passing the house to walk down path to the side of the house passed the garden. Then continue to follow path downhill to exit via a kissing gate opposite Wenlock Priory, then turn left back into the car park area.

Chapter 8 Beckbury

Park & Start Grid ref; SJ 764015

Distance: 3.25 miles

Level; Easy

Time: 1 hours 30 minutes

Terrain: Country lanes, paddocks and open fields.

Maps. O.S Explorer 242 Telford, Ironbridge and The Wrekin

Refreshments Seven Stars Inn Beckbury.

Amber dog on the trail in Beckbury.

Higford Mill

Access to start

Leave M54 motorway at junction 4 exit at 1st turn on roundabout onto A464, then at next roundabout take 3rd exit and follow A464 into Shifnal. Continue through the traffic lights in Shifnal and follow A464 and signpost on into Beckbury and park on the road near the church.

Places Nearby

Lichfield Cathedral

This is a magnificent building both inside and out, within easy reach nearby of restaurants and coffee shops. Along with the walk in Beckbury a truly brilliant day.

The Walk

(1)

The walk starts by parking on the lane near the church. Then walk into the churchyard and past the church on the path to the right, then just follow path up to the mall gate tucked away in the right corner, once through the gate cross the stile into a field. Keep over to the right to continue along a well-defined path with Beckbury Hall off to the right. Carry on along the path and at way marker continue straight ahead to drop down a slope to enter another field, stay straight ahead along the boundary path with a woodland off to the left. Then cross a stile to go down stone steps and at the bottom go left to continue straight on around the field boundary. Then after a short distance when the edge of the field goes right, keep over to the left up a well-defined path through a woodland on into a field.

(2)

Once in the field continue through the arable field carry straight on past a pylon to finally reach an open gateway by a tree. At this point go right down a slope following the wide track to the bottom of field, then uphill on the other side turn right with the hedge in front. Now continue to follow the field boundary in which it zigs and zags around the boundary perimeter to finally reach a footpath off to the left which then descends into the woods.

(3)

Once on the path just continue to follow the path straight on through the woods which runs in parallel with small tributary that feeds into the River Worfe, just go straight ahead to come out by the Higford Mill and cottages. Go through open area between mill and cottages to follow the road uphill and on past the entrance to Higford Hall. Then just continue to follow the lane straight on for about half a mile to reach a road junction to turn right onto the Beckbury lane.

(4)

Stay on the lane and when it drops downhill you can take the track off to the right onto a bridleway, but at the time of walk it was slightly overgrown. So as an easy alternative stay on the quiet country lane for almost a mile to a road junction, turn right at junction and follow lane back into Beckbury. Go past the Seven Stars Inn on through the village back to the parked car.

Chapter 9 Wrekin

Park & Start Grid ref; SJ 638092

Distance: 3 miles

Level; Strenuous

Time: 2 hours

Terrain: Step hill path and woodland tracks.

Maps. O.S Explorer 242 Telford, Ironbridge and The Wrekin

Refreshments Wrekin seasonal only.

Path uphill to top of Wrekin

Downhill track off the Wrekin.

Access to start

Leave the M54 motorway at junction 7, and then at the bottom of the slip road turn left and follow road up to a car park on the left in a disused quarry.

Places Nearby

The Dana Prison Shrewsbury

This is a fun and great place with its creepy corridors, odd cells and staff dressed as prisoners to scare the life out of you all in the name of fun? The staff are all great fun, but please beware that it is very cold inside the prison even in the summer months.

The Walk

(1)

The walk starts at the car park off to the left in the disused quarry. Exit car park to carefully cross the road and turn right heading for a road junction a few metres down the road and turn left. Then almost immediately just off the road junction turn left onto a track that quickly starts to rise into the woods. Keep following the track as it lazily twists and turns uphill for about half a mile. Just continue to follow main track as it veers sharply to the right ignoring the narrower path that goes away to the left.

(2)

Carry on your climb uphill still on the main track to pass by the Wrekin Cottage, a source of refreshment (can be open only seasonal) this is off to the right surrounded by a fence, this is almost halfway to the top. Continue through what was once a gateway still on the main track it continues to wind uphill and then around a left-hand hairpin bend, be sure to take in the views on the way to the top. Eventually you will reach the top at the trig pillar the climb is well worth it when you see the views out over a magnificent landscape.

(3)

So once at the top and you have enjoyed the views and rest to continue down go past the trig pillar down to a rocky outcrop on the left, at this point if you want to take a detour to the Needles Eye then take the path to left just past the rocks which runs down around and under the rocks. But for the walk just stay on the main track which soon drops away very steeply downhill and shortly enters the woodland area. Just continue to follow the path as it drops away taking care it can be slippery at times and certain places and it does get very steep. Continue downhill to reach a track at the bottom that is a permissive pathway, turn left here and continue to follow path to the end to reach a junction after about a mile with a marker pointing back the way you have come with permissive path marked on it.

(4)

Once at this point turn left onto a main track and then follow track for almost a mile to finally reach a slight uphill section to go up to a junction. At this point you have arrived back via the narrow path to where you go uphill to the Wrekin Cottage. We turn right and then follow the track back downhill to the road, then retrace your steps carefully back to the car park.

Chapter 10 Tong

Park & Start Grid ref; SJ 796074

Distance: 3.5 miles

Level; Easy

Time: 1 hours 30 minutes

Terrain: Open paddocks, fields, green lanes and country lanes.

Maps. O.S Explorer 242 Telford, Ironbridge and The Wrekin

Refreshments Albrighton.

Through the country at Tong.

Beautiful style houses in Tong.

Access to start

Leave M54 motorway at junction 3 and take the slip road to A41 towards Wolverhampton, then at the roundabout take 1st exit onto A41 Newport Road into Tong to park near the church on the road.

Places Nearby

St Bartholomew's Church Tong

This is worth the visit a beautiful church with many centuries of local Christian history. Check out the Golden Chapel and see the fictitious grave of Little Neil, the character from Charles Dickens the Old Curiosity Shop.

The Walk

(1)

The walk starts on road near to the church, park on lane here and then facing the church go left on opposite side of lane and follow the pavement through the village taking in the delightful variation of houses along the way. Once reaching the end of the village the road then swings around to the right towards a road junction with the A41, but just before the bend go off to the left onto a concrete driveway. Follow the drive for almost half mile to come to a fork on drive. All the markers point to go to the right, but we turn left heading to the Tong Farm Livery. At the livery buildings go straight ahead on past farm buildings on left, then on reaching the last brick built building turn right down on an enclosed track between paddocks follow a short distance to the end.

(2)

After reaching the end go through the gateway and turn left to follow the hedge on the left along a wide track with paddocks off to the right. Stay on this track to go through another gate, keep the hedge to your left and follow the track to reach a gateway with a tree lined pond just over to the left. Then go through the gateway ahead and follow the track up through the next field with the hedge on the right, carry straight ahead into the next field and then follow the track to a gateway at the end of field.

(3)

Go through the gateway and turn left at a crossroads of footpaths continue straight ahead on the green lane which will take you back into Tong after about a mile. Once on the green lane lookout for the views out to the Wrekin and Lizard Hill and across the Weston Estate. Continue to follow the green lane on past Tong Hill Farm which at this point changes into a metalled lane which you carry on following to enter the village just opposite the church to the parked car.

More Information on the Meandering Walking Series Paperbacks.

Meandering in Mid Devon
Meandering in South Devon
Meandering on Rivers and Canals in Devon
Meandering Pub Walks in Devon
Meandering Tea Rooms Walks in Devon
Meandering in Gloucestershire
Meandering on the Exe Estuary Trail
Meandering Through History, Mysteries or Legends in Devon
Meandering Pub Walks in Gloucestershire
Meandering with Man's Best Friend in Devon
Meandering the Severn Vale
Meandering More Pub Walks in Devon
Meandering in Lincolnshire
Meandering the South Hams
Meandering in Shropshire
Meandering in Dorset (January 2018)
Meandering in East Devon (April 2018)
Meandering in Somerset (2018)
Meandering the Countryside and Coast in Devon (2019)
Meandering in Worcestershire (2019)
Checkout some of the photos from the Meandering Walking Series

John Coombes google plus

Website:

http://johncoombes.wix.com/meandering-walks-2

Much Wenlock Priory

Printed in Great Britain
by Amazon